EMMANUEL JOSEPH

Strategic Synergy, Unveiling the Business Approaches of Valley Innovators and Property Magnates

Copyright © 2025 by Emmanuel Joseph

All rights reserved. No part of this publication may be reproduced, stored or transmitted in any form or by any means, electronic, mechanical, photocopying, recording, scanning, or otherwise without written permission from the publisher. It is illegal to copy this book, post it to a website, or distribute it by any other means without permission.

First edition

*This book was professionally typeset on Reedsy.
Find out more at reedsy.com*

Contents

1	Chapter 1: The Dawn of Innovation	1
2	Chapter 2: The Rise of Property Magnates	3
3	Chapter 3: Strategic Synergy in Action	5
4	Chapter 4: The Role of Venture Capital	7
5	Chapter 5: The Impact of Technology on Real Estate	9
6	Chapter 6: Building Sustainable Communities	11
7	Chapter 7: The Role of Leadership in Innovation	13
8	Chapter 8: The Intersection of Technology and Real Estate	15
9	Chapter 9: Overcoming Challenges and Adversity	17
10	Chapter 10: The Future of Strategic Synergy	19
11	Chapter 11: Case Studies in Strategic Synergy	21
12	Chapter 12: Lessons Learned and the Path Forward	23

1

Chapter 1: The Dawn of Innovation

In the early days of Silicon Valley, the landscape was vastly different from the bustling hub of technology it is today. A handful of visionaries saw potential in the rolling hills and quiet suburbs of Northern California. These early pioneers were not deterred by the lack of infrastructure or the skepticism of traditional business magnates. Instead, they were driven by a relentless belief in the power of technology to transform lives and industries. They established the first tech companies in the garages and basements of their homes, laying the foundation for what would become a global phenomenon.

As the valley began to attract more talent, a culture of collaboration emerged. Innovators shared ideas and resources, understanding that their collective success depended on the synergy of their efforts. This spirit of cooperation fostered an environment where groundbreaking technologies could flourish. It was during this time that some of the most influential companies of the modern era were born. These companies not only revolutionized the tech industry but also set the standard for business practices and corporate culture.

The growth of Silicon Valley was not without its challenges. The pioneers faced numerous obstacles, including financial constraints, regulatory hurdles, and intense competition. However, their unwavering determination and ability to adapt to changing circumstances allowed them to overcome these challenges. They learned to navigate the complex landscape of venture capital and formed strategic partnerships that provided the necessary support for their ventures. This period of growth and adaptation laid the groundwork for the valley's eventual dominance in the tech world.

The success of Silicon Valley caught the attention of investors and entrepreneurs from around the globe. As word spread, the valley became a magnet for talent and capital. The influx of new ideas and resources further accelerated the pace of innovation. It was during this time that the concept of "strategic synergy" began to take shape. Business leaders recognized the importance of aligning their efforts to achieve common goals. This collaborative approach became a hallmark of Silicon Valley's success and a key factor in its sustained growth.

Today, Silicon Valley stands as a testament to the power of innovation and collaboration. The early pioneers laid the foundation for a thriving ecosystem that continues to drive technological advancements. Their legacy is not only evident in the success of the companies they founded but also in the enduring culture of strategic synergy that defines the valley. As we move forward, it is essential to remember the lessons of these early innovators and continue to embrace the collaborative spirit that has made Silicon Valley a global leader in technology and business.

2

Chapter 2: The Rise of Property Magnates

While Silicon Valley was establishing itself as the epicenter of technological innovation, a parallel revolution was taking place in the world of real estate. Visionary property magnates recognized the potential for growth and transformation in urban landscapes. They understood that the success of technology companies would create a demand for modern infrastructure and housing. These magnates embarked on ambitious projects that would reshape cities and create new opportunities for economic development.

The property magnates were strategic in their approach, leveraging their expertise and resources to develop innovative real estate solutions. They focused on creating sustainable, mixed-use developments that catered to the needs of both businesses and residents. These developments not only provided state-of-the-art facilities for tech companies but also offered a high quality of life for employees and their families. The integration of technology and real estate became a key driver of urban growth and revitalization.

One of the defining characteristics of the property magnates was their ability to anticipate trends and adapt to changing market conditions. They were quick to recognize the impact of technological advancements on the real estate industry and sought to incorporate these innovations into their projects. From smart buildings to green technologies, the property magnates were at the forefront of creating sustainable and efficient urban environments. Their forward-thinking approach helped to set new standards for the industry and attract a new generation of real estate professionals.

The rise of property magnates was also marked by a focus on collaboration and strategic partnerships. They understood that the success of their projects depended on the ability to work closely with technology companies, local governments, and community organizations. By fostering strong relationships with these stakeholders, the property magnates were able to secure the necessary support and resources for their ventures. This collaborative approach not only facilitated the development of large-scale projects but also ensured that they met the needs of the communities they served.

As the property magnates continued to push the boundaries of innovation, they left a lasting impact on the urban landscape. Their projects transformed cities into vibrant hubs of economic activity and cultural exchange. The legacy of these visionaries can be seen in the thriving neighborhoods and state-of-the-art facilities that define modern urban living. Their contributions to the real estate industry have set the stage for future growth and development, ensuring that cities remain dynamic and resilient in the face of change.

3

Chapter 3: Strategic Synergy in Action

The concept of strategic synergy became a driving force in both Silicon Valley and the real estate industry. Business leaders from both sectors recognized the value of aligning their efforts to achieve common goals. This approach not only enhanced their individual successes but also created a powerful ecosystem of innovation and growth. By working together, tech companies and property developers were able to create environments that fostered creativity, collaboration, and productivity.

One of the key strategies for achieving strategic synergy was the creation of technology parks and innovation hubs. These developments provided state-of-the-art facilities for tech companies, as well as amenities that catered to the needs of their employees. By integrating technology and real estate, these hubs became incubators for new ideas and ventures. The close proximity of companies allowed for the rapid exchange of knowledge and resources, accelerating the pace of innovation.

Another important aspect of strategic synergy was the focus on sustainability. Both tech companies and property developers understood the importance of creating environmentally friendly and energy-efficient solutions. By incorporating green technologies into their projects, they were able to reduce their environmental impact and attract environmentally conscious investors and consumers. This commitment to sustainability not only enhanced their reputations but also created long-term value for their stakeholders.

Strategic partnerships between tech companies and property developers also played a crucial role in their success. By working together, they were able to leverage their respective strengths and resources to create innovative solutions. These partnerships often involved joint ventures, co-investments, and collaborative research and development efforts. By pooling their expertise and resources, they were able to tackle complex challenges and create value for their customers and communities.

The success of strategic synergy was not limited to Silicon Valley and urban real estate. The principles of collaboration and innovation were adopted by business leaders around the world. Companies in diverse industries began to recognize the value of aligning their efforts to achieve common goals. This shift in mindset led to the creation of new business models and strategies that emphasized the importance of collaboration and strategic partnerships. As a result, the concept of strategic synergy became a cornerstone of modern business practices.

4

Chapter 4: The Role of Venture Capital

Venture capital played a critical role in the success of Silicon Valley and the real estate industry. These investors provided the necessary funding and support for early-stage companies and ambitious real estate projects. Venture capitalists were not only financial backers but also strategic partners, offering valuable guidance and resources to help entrepreneurs navigate the complex landscape of business development.

One of the key factors that set Silicon Valley apart was its robust ecosystem of venture capital. The region attracted investors from around the world, drawn by the promise of high returns and the opportunity to be part of the next big thing. This influx of capital provided the necessary fuel for innovation, allowing startups to scale rapidly and bring their groundbreaking ideas to market. The close-knit community of investors and entrepreneurs fostered a culture of collaboration and risk-taking, which became a hallmark of Silicon Valley's success.

In the real estate industry, venture capital played a similar role in driving innovation and growth. Property developers relied on these investors to fund large-scale projects and bring their visionary ideas to life. Venture capitalists provided not only financial support but also strategic guidance, helping developers navigate the complex regulatory landscape and secure the necessary approvals and permits. This partnership allowed developers to take on ambitious projects that would have been impossible without the backing of venture capital.

The relationship between venture capitalists and entrepreneurs was built on mutual trust and a shared vision for the future. Investors were willing to take risks on unproven ideas and disruptive technologies, understanding that failure was an inherent part of the innovation process. This willingness to embrace uncertainty allowed entrepreneurs to experiment and push the boundaries of what was possible. In return, successful ventures provided significant returns on investment, creating a cycle of reinvestment and continuous innovation.

As Silicon Valley and the real estate industry continued to evolve, the role of venture capital remained crucial. Investors adapted to changing market conditions and emerging trends, seeking out new opportunities for growth and innovation. The success of these ventures not only benefited the investors but also created a positive impact on the broader economy. By supporting the next generation of innovators and developers, venture capitalists played a vital role in shaping the future of technology and urban development.

5

Chapter 5: The Impact of Technology on Real Estate

The rapid advancement of technology had a profound impact on the real estate industry. From smart buildings to virtual reality, tech innovations transformed the way properties were developed, managed, and marketed. Property developers and real estate professionals embraced these technologies to create more efficient, sustainable, and attractive solutions for their clients and communities.

One of the most significant advancements was the development of smart buildings. These structures were equipped with sensors, automation systems, and advanced analytics that allowed for real-time monitoring and control of various building functions. From energy management to security, smart buildings provided enhanced efficiency and convenience for both occupants and property managers. This technology not only reduced operational costs but also improved the overall experience for residents and tenants.

Virtual reality (VR) and augmented reality (AR) also revolutionized the real estate industry. These technologies allowed potential buyers and tenants to explore properties remotely, providing immersive and interactive experiences. VR and AR made it possible to visualize and customize spaces before they were built, reducing the risk of costly design changes and ensuring that projects met the needs and preferences of clients. This innovation streamlined the sales and leasing process, making it more efficient and customer-centric.

The integration of technology also extended to property management and maintenance. Advanced software solutions allowed property managers to streamline operations, track maintenance schedules, and communicate with tenants more effectively. Predictive analytics and IoT devices enabled proactive maintenance, identifying potential issues before they became major problems. This approach not only improved the longevity and performance of buildings but also enhanced tenant satisfaction and retention.

Technology also played a crucial role in the design and construction of sustainable buildings. Green technologies, such as solar panels, energy-efficient HVAC systems, and water-saving fixtures, were integrated into new developments to reduce their environmental impact. Property developers used advanced modeling and simulation tools to optimize building performance and minimize resource consumption. This commitment to sustainability not only attracted environmentally conscious investors and tenants but also created long-term value for all stakeholders.

The impact of technology on real estate was far-reaching, transforming every aspect of the industry. By embracing innovation and leveraging new technologies, property developers and real estate professionals were able to create more efficient, sustainable, and customer-centric solutions. This ongoing evolution ensured that the industry remained dynamic and resilient in the face of change, driving continued growth and development.

6

Chapter 6: Building Sustainable Communities

As the world faced growing environmental challenges, the importance of sustainability in real estate became increasingly evident. Property developers and urban planners recognized the need to create communities that were not only economically viable but also environmentally responsible and socially inclusive. This shift in focus led to the development of sustainable communities that prioritized the well-being of both people and the planet.

Sustainable communities were designed with a holistic approach, considering factors such as energy efficiency, resource conservation, and social equity. These developments incorporated green building practices and technologies to reduce their environmental impact. From renewable energy sources to green roofs and rainwater harvesting systems, sustainable communities embraced innovative solutions to minimize their carbon footprint and promote ecological balance.

In addition to environmental sustainability, these communities also prioritized social inclusivity and accessibility. Property developers worked closely with local governments and community organizations to ensure that their projects met the needs of diverse populations. This included providing affordable housing options, creating public spaces for social interaction, and designing accessible infrastructure for people of all abilities. By fostering a sense of community and belonging, these developments aimed to create vibrant and resilient neighborhoods.

Economic sustainability was another key aspect of building sustainable communities. Property developers and urban planners focused on creating mixed-use developments that integrated residential, commercial, and recreational spaces. This approach not only reduced the need for long commutes but also supported local businesses and economic growth. By creating self-sufficient communities, these developments contributed to the overall resilience and sustainability of urban areas.

The success of sustainable communities relied on collaboration and strategic partnerships. Property developers, local governments, and community organizations worked together to achieve common goals and address complex challenges. This collaborative approach ensured that projects were well-planned and executed, meeting the needs of both current and future generations. By prioritizing sustainability, these communities set a new standard for urban development and created a positive impact on the environment and society.

As the world continued to grapple with environmental and social challenges, the importance of building sustainable communities became even more critical. The lessons learned from these developments provided valuable insights and best practices for future projects. By embracing sustainability and collaboration, property developers and urban planners could create communities that were not only successful but also resilient and thriving in the face of change.

7

Chapter 7: The Role of Leadership in Innovation

Leadership played a crucial role in the success of both Silicon Valley and the real estate industry. Visionary leaders were able to inspire and guide their teams, fostering a culture of innovation and collaboration. Their ability to navigate complex challenges and make strategic decisions was instrumental in driving the growth and success of their ventures.

One of the key qualities of effective leaders was their ability to inspire and motivate their teams. They created a shared vision and set ambitious goals, encouraging their employees to think creatively and take risks. By fostering a culture of innovation, these leaders empowered their teams to push the boundaries of what was possible. This approach not only drove technological advancements but also created a sense of purpose and fulfillment among employees.

Effective leaders also demonstrated a strong commitment to collaboration and teamwork. They recognized that the success of their ventures depended on the collective efforts of their teams and partners. By promoting open communication and collaboration, these leaders created an environment where ideas could be freely shared and developed. This approach not only enhanced the quality of their projects but also strengthened relationships with stakeholders and partners.

Another important aspect of leadership was the ability to make strategic decisions in the face of uncertainty. Effective leaders were able to navigate complex challenges and adapt to changing market conditions. They demonstrated a willingness to take calculated risks and make bold moves, understanding that failure was an inherent part of the innovation process. This ability to make strategic decisions allowed them to make informed decisions and seize new opportunities.

A critical aspect of leadership in Silicon Valley was fostering a culture of continuous learning and development. Leaders encouraged their teams to stay abreast of the latest industry trends, invest in ongoing education, and pursue personal growth. This commitment to learning ensured that their teams remained at the cutting edge of technology and innovation. It also created an environment where employees felt valued and supported, contributing to higher levels of job satisfaction and retention.

The role of leadership in the real estate industry was equally important. Property developers and urban planners needed to navigate complex regulatory landscapes, secure financing, and manage large-scale projects. Effective leaders in this field demonstrated a keen understanding of market dynamics and a strong ability to build and maintain relationships with stakeholders. Their strategic vision and ability to execute complex projects were instrumental in driving the success of their ventures.

In both Silicon Valley and the real estate industry, effective leadership was characterized by a commitment to ethics and integrity. Leaders set the tone for their organizations by prioritizing transparency, accountability, and responsible business practices. This commitment to ethical leadership not only enhanced their reputations but also built trust with stakeholders and created a positive impact on their communities.

8

Chapter 8: The Intersection of Technology and Real Estate

The intersection of technology and real estate created new opportunities for innovation and growth. As tech companies and property developers collaborated, they developed solutions that transformed the way properties were designed, built, and managed. This convergence of industries led to the creation of smart cities, where technology was seamlessly integrated into the urban environment to enhance the quality of life for residents.

One of the most significant developments at this intersection was the rise of proptech (property technology) companies. These startups leveraged technology to solve challenges in the real estate industry, from property management to tenant engagement. Proptech innovations included digital platforms for buying, selling, and renting properties, as well as tools for automating property maintenance and operations. These solutions streamlined processes, improved efficiency, and provided greater transparency for all stakeholders.

Another important trend was the use of data analytics in real estate. Tech companies and property developers harnessed the power of big data to make informed decisions and optimize their projects. By analyzing data on market trends, tenant preferences, and building performance, they were able to create more effective strategies and deliver better outcomes. This data-driven approach also allowed for more accurate forecasting and risk management, reducing uncertainties and enhancing project success.

The integration of Internet of Things (IoT) devices into buildings and infrastructure was another key development. IoT technology enabled real-time monitoring and control of various building systems, from HVAC to lighting and security. This connectivity allowed property managers to optimize energy usage, enhance security, and provide a more comfortable and convenient experience for occupants. IoT also facilitated predictive maintenance, identifying potential issues before they became major problems and reducing downtime.

The collaboration between tech companies and property developers also led to the creation of smart city initiatives. These projects aimed to leverage technology to improve urban living, from transportation and infrastructure to public services and environmental sustainability. Smart cities integrated digital technologies into their urban fabric, creating connected and efficient environments that enhanced the quality of life for residents. These initiatives demonstrated the potential of strategic synergy to drive meaningful and lasting change in urban areas.

9

Chapter 9: Overcoming Challenges and Adversity

The journey to success for both Silicon Valley and the real estate industry was not without its challenges. Innovators and property magnates faced numerous obstacles, from financial constraints and regulatory hurdles to market volatility and intense competition. Their ability to overcome these challenges was a testament to their resilience, adaptability, and strategic thinking.

One of the most significant challenges for tech companies was securing funding and resources in the early stages. Many startups struggled to attract investors and gain traction in a competitive market. However, their perseverance and ability to pivot in response to changing circumstances allowed them to overcome these obstacles. By leveraging strategic partnerships and tapping into the supportive ecosystem of Silicon Valley, they were able to secure the necessary backing and achieve their goals.

Regulatory challenges also posed significant obstacles for both tech companies and property developers. Navigating complex regulations and obtaining the necessary approvals required a deep understanding of the legal landscape and strong relationships with regulatory authorities. Effective leaders in both industries demonstrated a keen ability to navigate these challenges, ensuring that their projects complied with regulations while still pushing the boundaries of innovation.

Market volatility was another major challenge. Economic downturns and shifting market dynamics created uncertainties that could derail even the most well-planned ventures. Innovators and property magnates demonstrated resilience by adapting their strategies and finding new opportunities in the face of adversity. Their ability to remain agile and responsive to changing market conditions was a key factor in their long-term success.

Intense competition also required business leaders to continuously innovate and differentiate their offerings. In Silicon Valley, the rapid pace of technological advancements meant that companies needed to stay ahead of the curve to remain relevant. Similarly, in the real estate industry, developers needed to create unique and attractive solutions to stand out in a crowded market. Their ability to innovate and deliver value to their customers was instrumental in overcoming competitive pressures.

The success of both Silicon Valley and the real estate industry was not just about overcoming challenges but also about learning from them. Business leaders used their experiences to refine their strategies, improve their operations, and build more resilient organizations. This commitment to continuous improvement ensured that they were well-equipped to navigate future challenges and seize new opportunities.

10

Chapter 10: The Future of Strategic Synergy

As we look to the future, the concept of strategic synergy will continue to play a crucial role in driving innovation and growth. The collaboration between tech companies and property developers will evolve to address emerging challenges and opportunities. New technologies, changing market dynamics, and shifting societal needs will shape the future of both industries, creating new possibilities for strategic synergy.

One of the key areas of focus will be the continued integration of technology into urban environments. Smart cities will become more prevalent, with technology playing an increasingly central role in enhancing the quality of life for residents. Innovations in areas such as transportation, energy management, and public services will create more efficient, sustainable, and connected urban environments. The collaboration between tech companies and property developers will be essential in realizing the full potential of smart cities.

Another important trend will be the rise of sustainable and resilient communities. As environmental and social challenges become more pressing, property developers and tech companies will need to work together to create solutions that address these issues. This will involve the development of green technologies, sustainable building practices, and inclusive urban planning.

By prioritizing sustainability and resilience, they will create communities that are better equipped to withstand future challenges and thrive in the long term.

The role of data and analytics will also become increasingly important. Tech companies and property developers will leverage advanced data analytics to gain deeper insights into market trends, tenant preferences, and building performance. This data-driven approach will enable more informed decision-making and optimize project outcomes. It will also facilitate the development of personalized and customer-centric solutions that meet the evolving needs of residents and businesses.

The future of strategic synergy will also be shaped by the ongoing evolution of business models and strategies. Companies in both industries will need to adapt to changing market conditions and embrace new approaches to collaboration and innovation. This may involve the development of new partnership models, the exploration of emerging technologies, and the adoption of agile and flexible business practices. By staying ahead of the curve and continuously innovating, they will ensure their continued success and growth.

11

Chapter 11: Case Studies in Strategic Synergy

To illustrate the power of strategic synergy, we can look at several case studies that highlight successful collaborations between tech companies and property developers. These examples demonstrate how strategic partnerships have driven innovation, created value, and transformed urban environments.

One notable case study is the development of a major technology park in Silicon Valley. This project brought together a leading tech company and a visionary property developer to create a state-of-the-art innovation hub. The technology park featured cutting-edge facilities, sustainable design elements, and amenities that catered to the needs of tech professionals. By leveraging their respective strengths, the partners were able to create a dynamic and collaborative environment that attracted top talent and fostered innovation.

Another example is the transformation of an urban district into a smart city. This project involved collaboration between multiple stakeholders, including tech companies, property developers, local governments, and community organizations. The smart city initiative integrated advanced technologies such as IoT, data analytics, and renewable energy to create a connected and sustainable urban environment. This collaborative approach not only enhanced the quality of life for residents but also set a new standard for urban development.

A third case study focuses on the development of a mixed-use community that prioritized sustainability and inclusivity. The property developer and tech company worked together to create a community that incorporated green building practices, affordable housing options, and accessible infrastructure. This project demonstrated the potential of strategic synergy to address pressing environmental and social challenges while creating economic value.

These case studies highlight the importance of collaboration, innovation, and strategic thinking in achieving successful outcomes. They demonstrate how strategic synergy can drive meaningful and lasting change in urban environments, creating value for all stakeholders and setting the stage for future growth and development.

12

Chapter 12: Lessons Learned and the Path Forward

As we reflect on the success of Silicon Valley and the real estate industry, several key lessons emerge that can guide future efforts in achieving strategic synergy. These lessons highlight the importance of innovation, collaboration, and adaptability in driving growth and success.

One of the most important lessons is the value of a collaborative mindset. Business leaders in both industries recognized that their success depended on the collective efforts of their teams and partners. By fostering a culture of collaboration and open communication, they were able to harness the power of strategic synergy and achieve common goals. This collaborative approach will continue to be essential in addressing future challenges and seizing new opportunities.

Another key lesson is the importance of embracing innovation and staying ahead of the curve. The rapid pace of technological advancements and changing market dynamics require companies to continuously innovate and adapt. By investing in research and development, staying abreast of industry trends, and encouraging creative thinking, business leaders can ensure that their organizations remain at the cutting edge of innovation.

The ability to navigate challenges and adapt to changing circumstances is another crucial lesson. Both Silicon Valley innovators and property magnates faced numerous obstacles on their journey to success. Their ability to remain resilient and flexible allowed them to overcome these challenges and turn them into opportunities. This mindset of adaptability will continue to be essential in navigating future uncertainties and achieving long-term success.

A commitment to sustainability and social responsibility is also a key takeaway. Business leaders in both industries recognized the importance of creating environmentally friendly and socially inclusive solutions. By prioritizing sustainability and social equity, they were able to create value for their stakeholders and contribute to the well-being of their communities. This focus on responsible business practices will be increasingly important in addressing the pressing challenges of the future.

As we move forward, the principles of strategic synergy will continue to guide the efforts of tech companies, property developers, and business leaders across industries. By embracing collaboration, innovation, and adaptability, they will be well-equipped to navigate the complex landscape of the future and create meaningful and lasting change. The lessons learned from the success of Silicon Valley and the real estate industry will provide valuable insights and inspiration for future endeavors.

In conclusion, "Strategic Synergy: Unveiling the Business Approaches of Valley Innovators and Property Magnates" highlights the power of collaboration and innovation in driving growth and success. The stories of Silicon Valley pioneers and visionary property magnates demonstrate the importance of strategic partnerships, forward-thinking leadership, and a commitment to sustainability. By embracing these principles, business leaders can create value for their stakeholders, transform urban environments, and shape the future of their industries. As we look to the future, the lessons learned from these trailblazers will continue to inspire and guide our efforts in achieving strategic synergy and driving meaningful change.

"Strategic Synergy: Unveiling the Business Approaches of Valley Innovators and Property Magnates" delves into the collaborative dynamics that have shaped Silicon Valley's tech giants and the real estate visionaries who transform urban landscapes. This book explores the intertwined stories of early tech pioneers and property magnates, revealing how their strategic

CHAPTER 12: LESSONS LEARNED AND THE PATH FORWARD

partnerships and innovative thinking have driven unprecedented growth and development.

Through twelve insightful chapters, the book examines the rise of Silicon Valley, the impact of technology on real estate, and the creation of sustainable communities. It highlights key themes such as the role of leadership, the influence of venture capital, and the integration of cutting-edge technologies into urban environments. By showcasing case studies and practical examples, the book illustrates how strategic synergy has become a cornerstone of modern business practices.

Whether you're an entrepreneur, investor, or simply curious about the forces driving innovation and urban transformation, "Strategic Synergy" offers valuable insights and lessons from the visionaries who have shaped our world. Join us on a journey through the history, challenges, and future possibilities of strategic collaboration and discover how synergy can create lasting impact and success.

www.ingramcontent.com/pod-product-compliance
Lightning Source LLC
LaVergne TN
LVHW020743090526
838202LV00057BA/6217